AF266213

to the ones who move between worlds
and linger near the veil

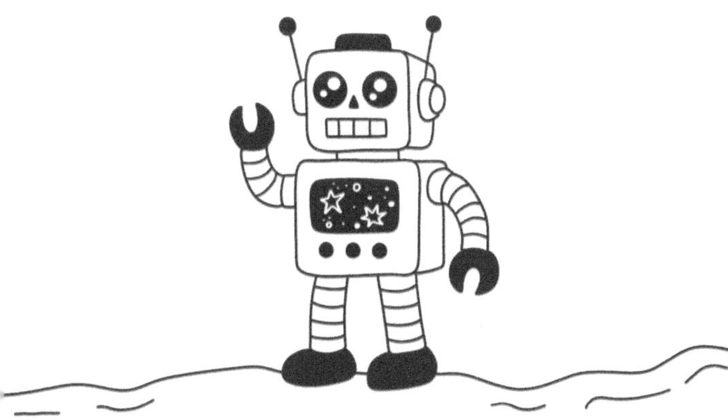

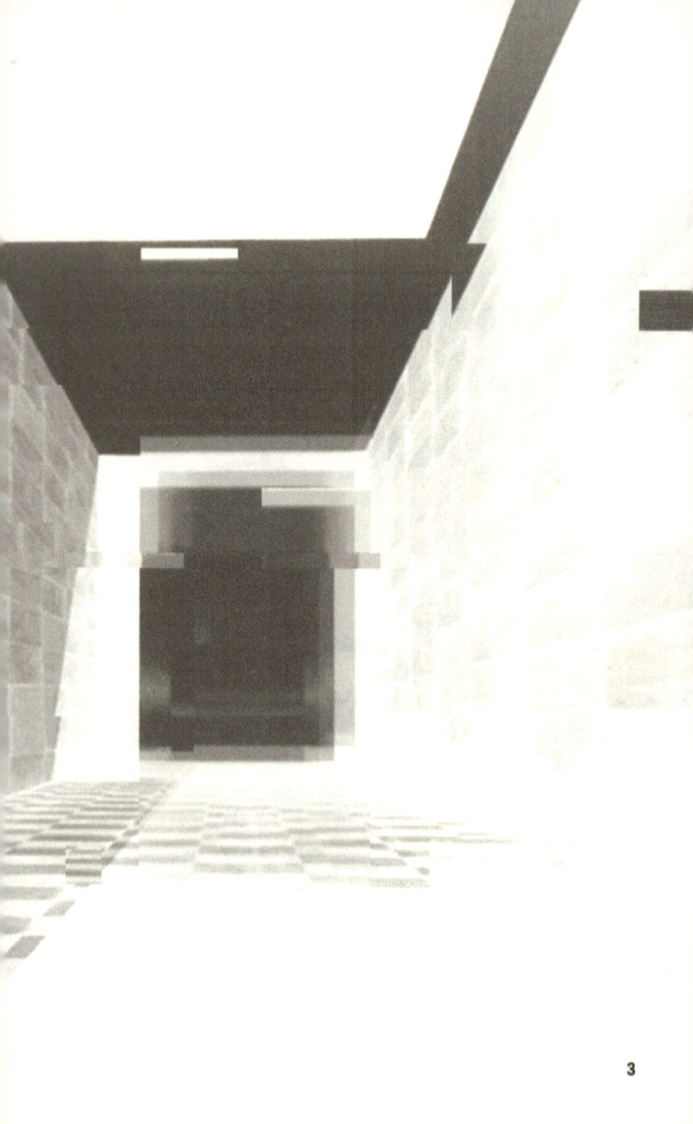

the fragile light of morning stars

poems about love and life
in liminal
spaces

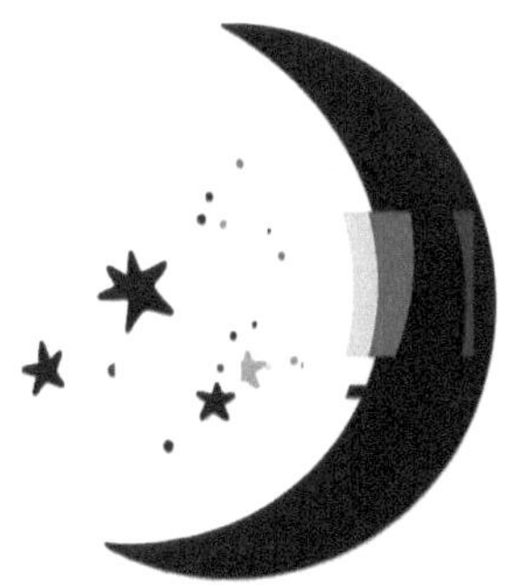

everything will be okay in the end...

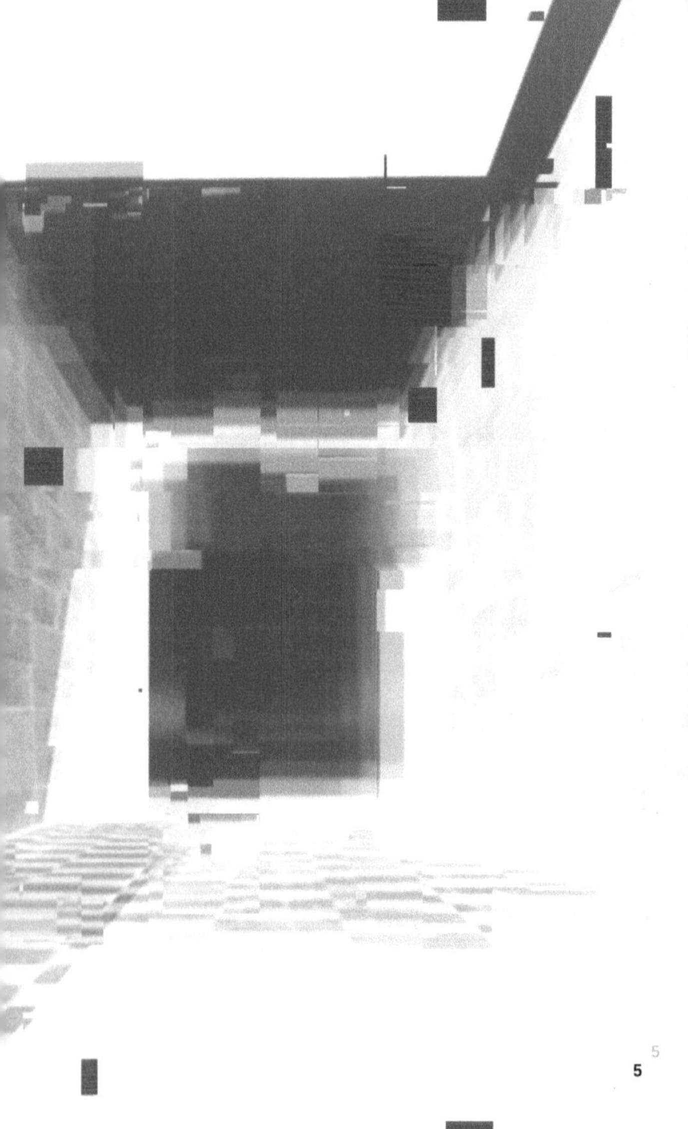

if it's not okay...

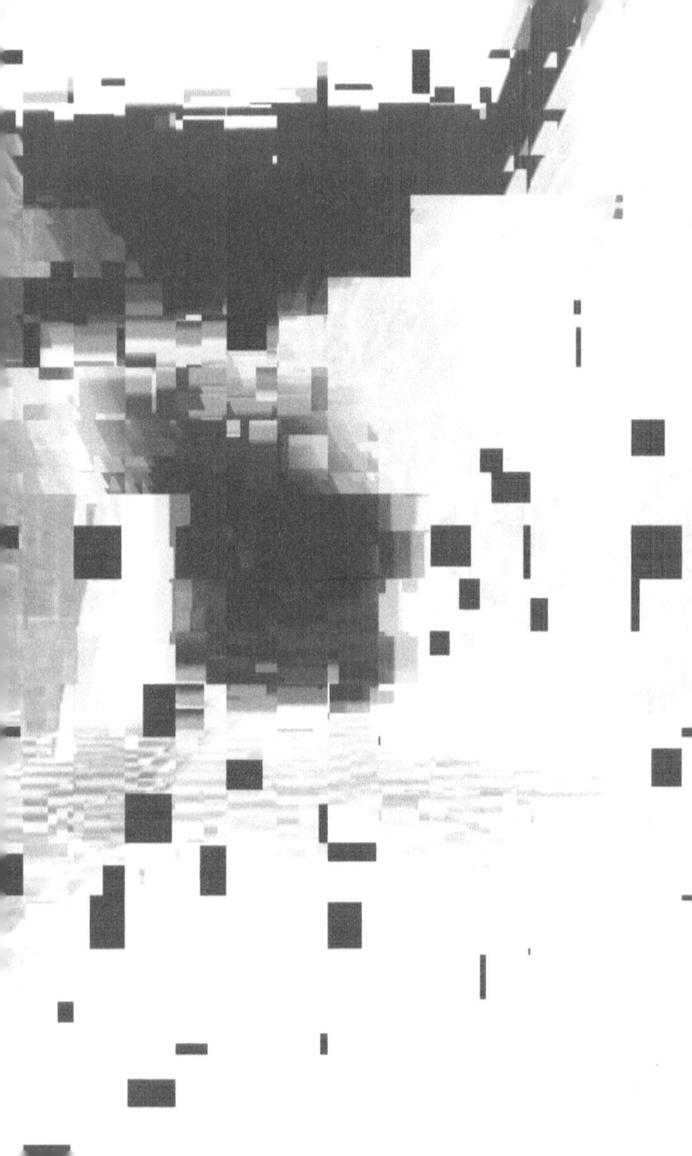

it's not the end.

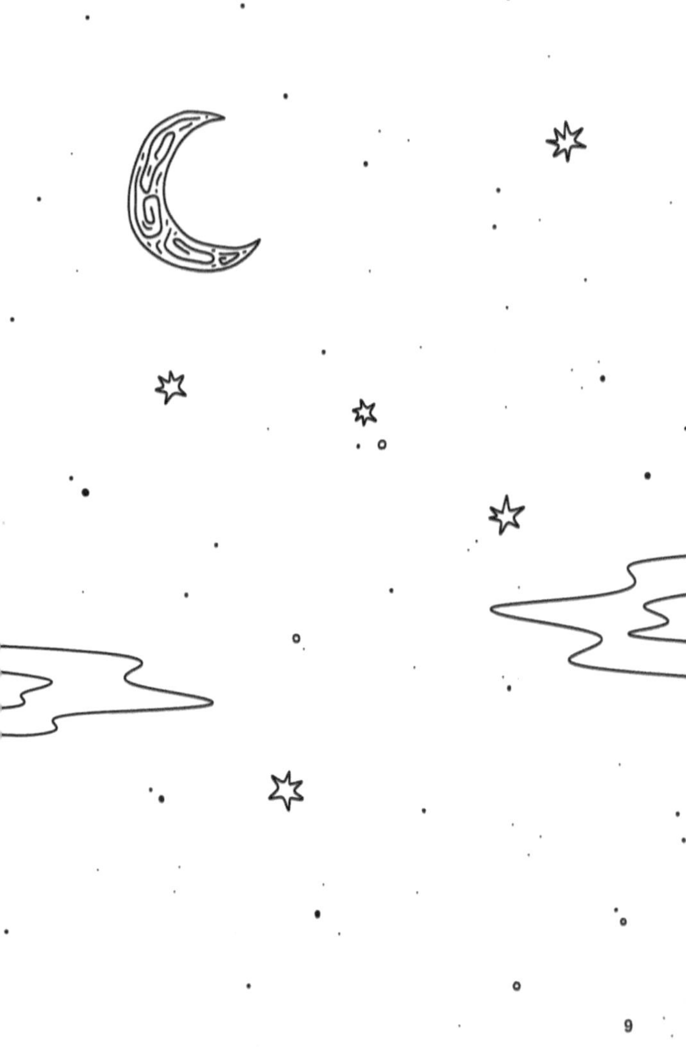

contents:

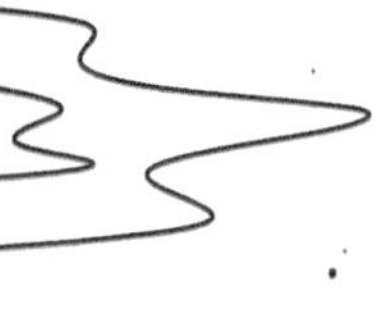

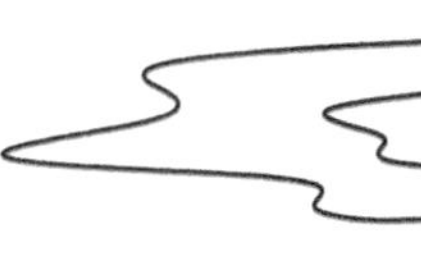

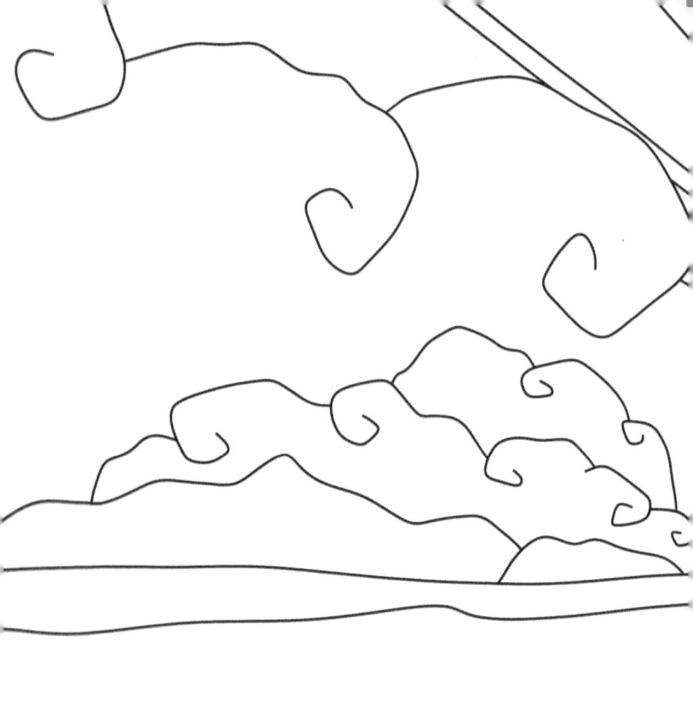

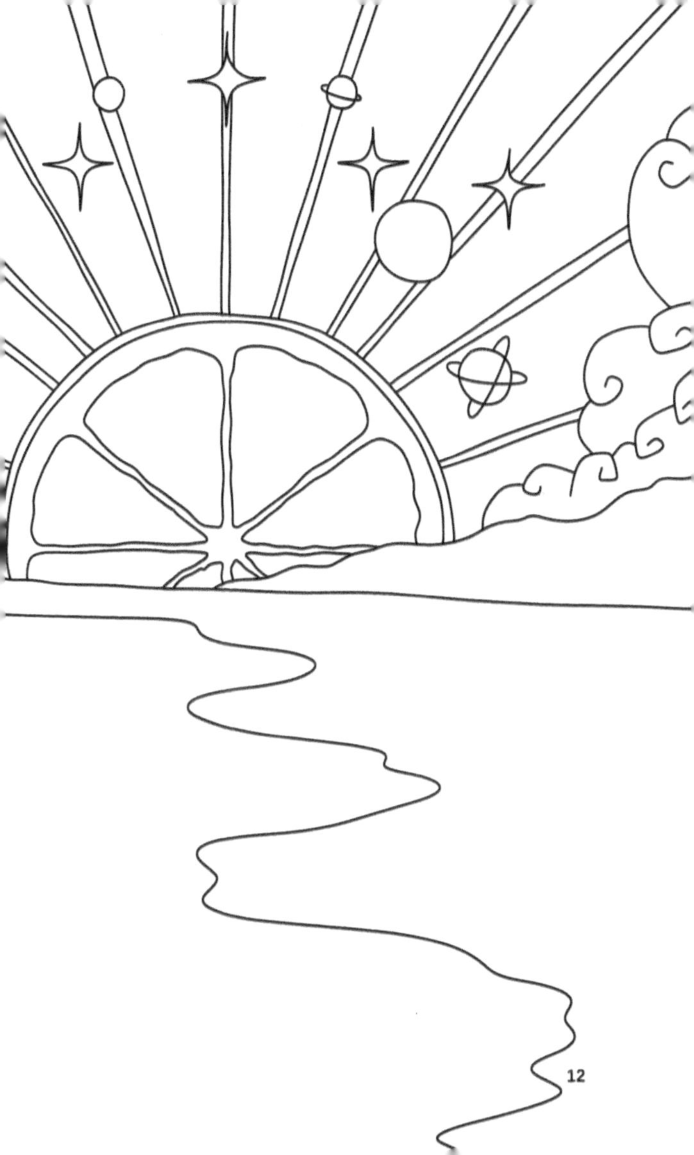

OUT OF BODY & KIND...

you'rescreaminngint othevoid...tiredasyou wanderthroughtheee recessesofthemind... avoidthetruth...letttt thepasttakehol...don' tgiveintoexperience... theresacertaincalmin theaftermathoffury... whatwillyou...wherew illyougonextyouaremi sunderstoodasyoutry tocommunicatwhyyo uleft...theresnevergoi ngtobeanotherwayth anthis...youfall||||||||||||

there's a different kind of madness
that comes at night:
do you know it?

something happens in the absence of light
that makes me feel alive
i thrive in the darkness
the gloom
the fog
others might get bogged down
by the cold shadows
that come out to play
but to me they are home
i beg them to stay
they give me inspiration
and comfort
and air
they tell me the truth
when there's no one there

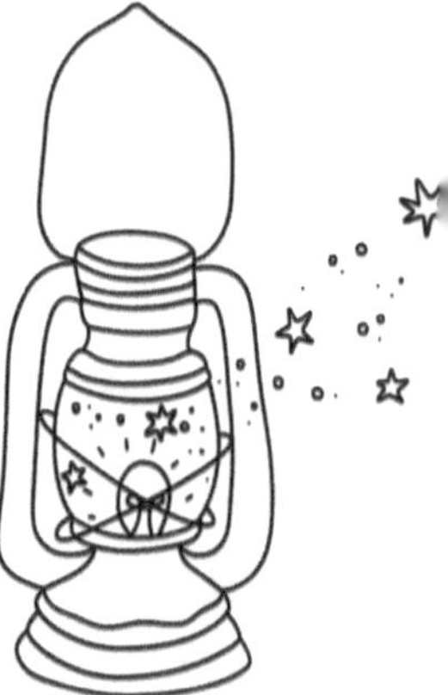

in the dark i find peace
and i can finally see
because there's no one around
and i can be me

i am not mad
i am finally free

08-2?-09
00:00 EDT
43.6510° N, '79.3470° W

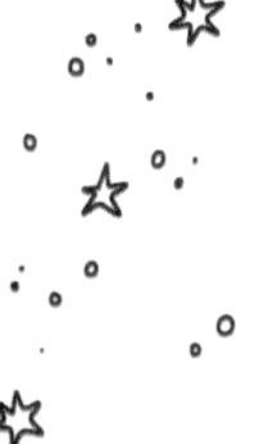

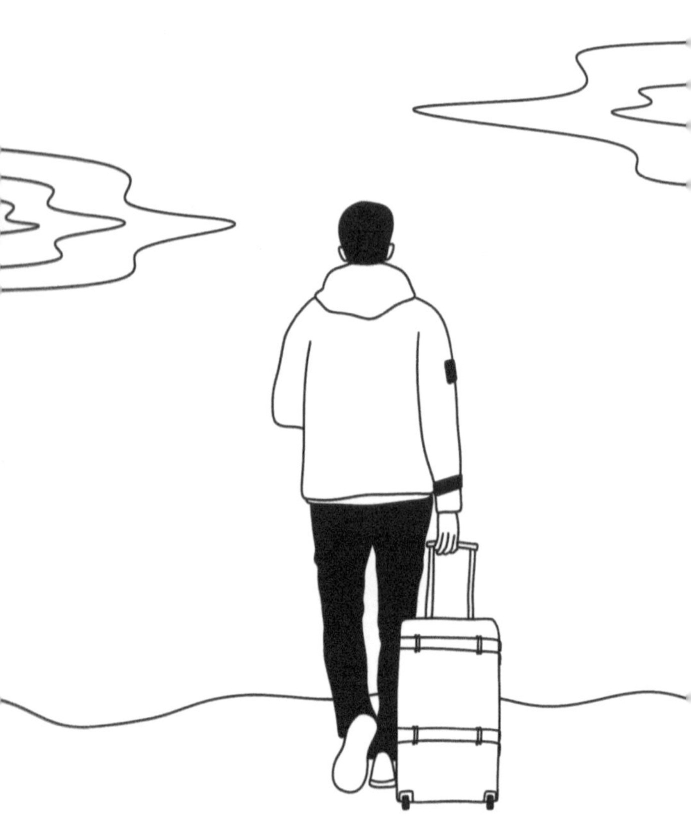

i started on this train of thought
more eager than i should
and now i'm drifting off to space
i feel misunderstood
my words they briefly cling the air
then fall to the spaces between
you're giving me a hard blank stare
and you don't know what i mean
i'm dearly grasping on to place
and time and circumstance
but something left me with no trace
and i am in a trance

[dissociating]

07-19-20
09.67 ES
42.5r55N'N, 79.3802° W
  3.64

you do not have to scream
at the top of your lungs
just to tell the truth
a whisper is fine
and actions more loud
but voiceless words
fall on blinded eyes
when you keep the company
of those who cannot see

[silent scream]

11-02-15
20:15 EST
45.4215° N, 75.6972° W

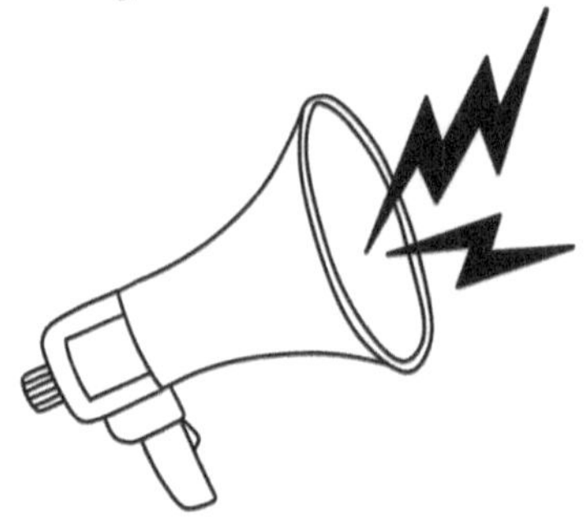

the lump you feel
in your throat
when you can't let go
of the tears
is the knowledge
that you are not
yet safe

trust that feeling

[choked up]

09-30-00
00:00 EDT
43.77_1° N, 79.2_78° W

as i'm clawing at the pages
my finger catches an edge
the words spill out like madness
as i teeter on the ledge
the insanity is stable
as i bleed my truth like wine
but something stops me in my tracks
and i can't find the line
i want to draw your attention
but my pen is out of ink
i try to write you pretty prose
but instead take up a drink

[writer's block]

10-31-02
22:45 EST
49.2827

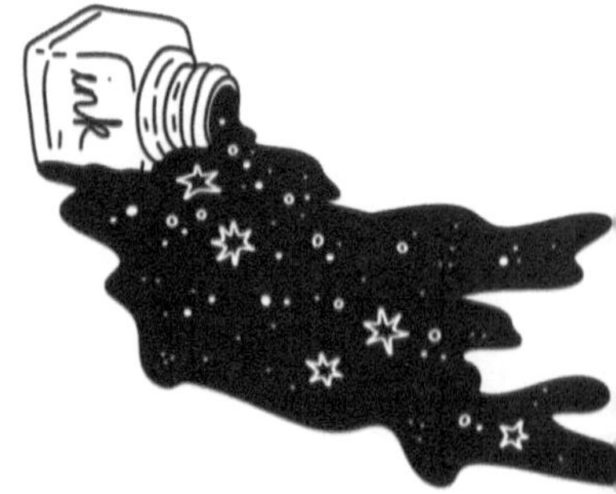

this potion
dulls the senses
all my edges
once rough
are now sanded smooth

i am tufted

i have become the wall
padding the home
of my latent shadow self

[relapse]

    ¦1
06-07-¬c1
^4:15 EST
46.8139° N, 71.2082° W

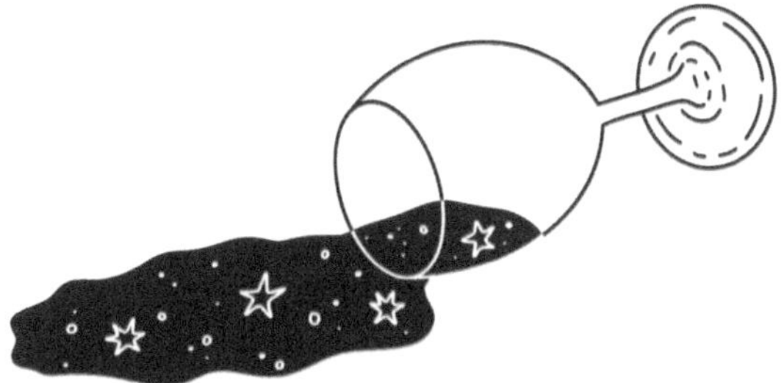

there are too many people here
herds of people
hordes of people
all doing the same thing

i want desperately to join them

they would like that too

but their movements
are foreign to me

their purpose eludes

i do not think
i will ever be the same

i mimic them for a while

how can i fit into a crowd
when i was always set apart
was i born to stand alone?

04-15-24
18:47 EST
40.7527° N, 73.9772° W

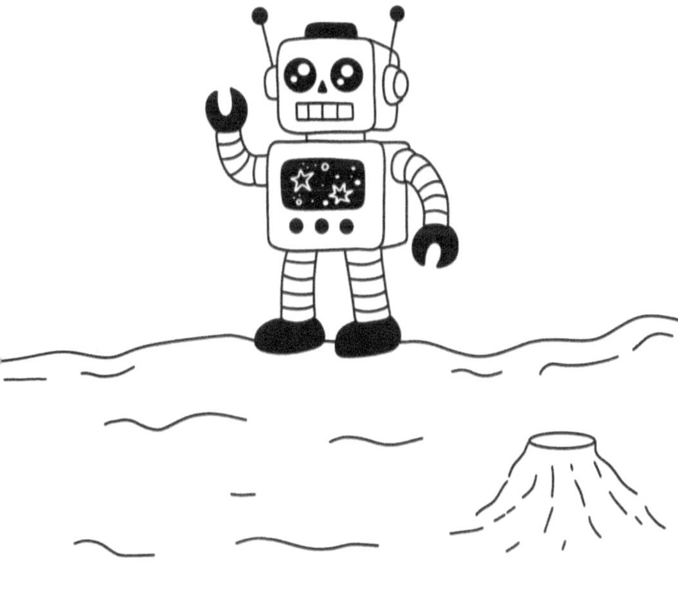

she combs the strands
of her coffee-colored hair
staring silently at herself
in the bathroom mirror

she is old and young
at the very same time

she makes faces at herself
in the window of her favorite shop
she's off to work and she won't stop
to go inside
all she wants to do is hide
and not think about the dress she eyed
because even though it is hard to admit
she knows that it will never fit

she dreams of who she might have been
if she wasn't afraid of being seen

surely something's got to give
and this is not a way to live
but the day is getting late
so she heads home at a quarter past 8
packing up her remaining sorrow
and prepares to feel the same tomorrow

[young mother]

09-14 5 3
20:15 66 ST
43.66° N, '79.3887° W

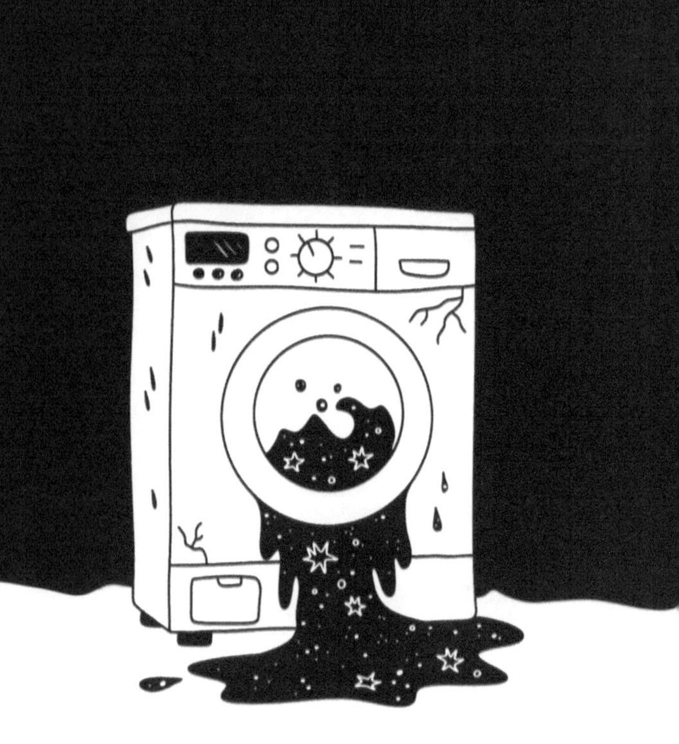

she was beautiful on her wedding day
but she needed so much more
to save her from the emptiness
of those who came before

her heart held the kind of hope
that only bares itself in youth
but wishes did not keep her warm
or save her from the truth

she was never her own person
and her fate was always set
she was silly in assuming
that her birth was not a debt

her dreams begin to leave her
as the sadness comes in waves
she lies between the cracks
inside the kitchen where she slaves

[young wife]

02-28 9
17:12 EST
45 4215 N, 75   19

what is the sound the soul makes
if no one is around to hear it

[illegible]
35.6871° N, 139.5558° E

stunned
shell-shocked
thick air fills my lungs
like half-hard glue
time is slowed to a leak
my thin heart shifts blood
to hollowed bones
you filled me up
and left me dry

tell me
in this fresh hell
how do i remold
the walls of a well
that's in your shape

i think i will die of thirst

[the day after love]

10-09-23
22:05 EST
^5.4215° N, ^5^6919° W

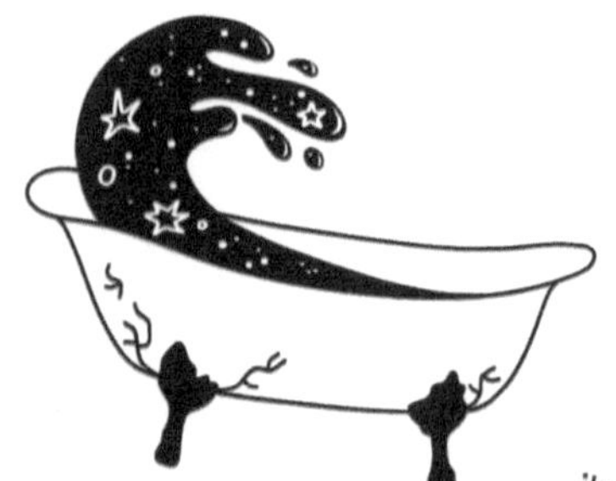

i'm in big trouble
but i am dimple-cheeked
and button-nosed

they tell me it's a good thing
the reason they didn't
toss the baby with the bathwater
when all hell broke loose

but now this neoteny deceives

they like the way i smile with my eyes
but i am wincing too

they cannot tell
that these are not laugh lines

05-06-24
15:18 EST
45.5017° N, 73.5673° W

3

please
misunderstand me
get me wrong
make many assumptions
about my character
tell the tribe
spread rumors
with your ignorant tongue
this is my preference
because every time you try to "get"
what i am about
i become a slave
to all the masks
you try to make me wear

08-28-23
23:50 EST
43.7768° N, 79.2310° W

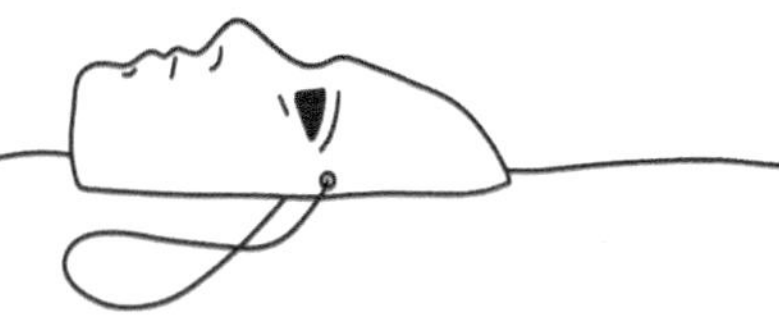

looking out two orbs of light
i see a strange old face
i'm told that it is just like mine
but have no proof to trace
am i in this avatar
or somewhere lost outside
i wonder how i got this view
then push those dreams aside

before the others notice me
i make my posture straight
and as i learn to walk their path
my footsteps match their gait

i think "this isn't so bad"
as i learn to speak their words
then i feel my being crack in halves
and quickly into thirds
then fourths and fifths and even more
while each one takes a slice
i have no say who gets what part
but perhaps this is the price
a debt i owe for being here
for sharing another's home
but if to break is to belong
at least i'm not alone

will i ever be whole again
it seems too late to ask
to hide my worry from their view
i'll wear this tiny mask
it's not so bad and fits quite well
except for the parts that sting
but there's company and i have no time
to allow my soul to sing

i learn to whisper to myself
as the years come rushing by
and as my memory starts to fail
tears fall down my eyes
i'm back where i once started
in the same stark crowded room
with the same familiar faces
and the same familiar gloom

through these cloudy orbs of light
i see a strange young face
i'm told that it is just like mine
but have no proof to trace
am i in this avatar
or somewhere in the sky
i wonder how i got this view
then breathe my final sigh

[the price of company]

i wish that my mind
were as tired as my body
i wish that my days
were as long as my dreams
i wish that the night
would come sooner not later
because of how out of place
this fantasy seems

[maladaptive daydreaming]

12-12-10
11:00 EST
44.2312° N, 76.4859° W

4

NOSTALGIA AND THE CITY

...placesandpeopleout
oftimeandspace...dej
avuinwaves...between
whereyouareandwher
eyou'regoing...memor
yislooooooongerthant
he...slowdownyoucraz
ychild...cracksinthegr
oundandcoldair.....cha
ngesinanewcity...losti
ntheplaceswhereweu
sedtobe...iisayyourna
meinthequiietstillnes
softhevoid...whatisha
ppeningtome.....where
haveyoube.....istilllove

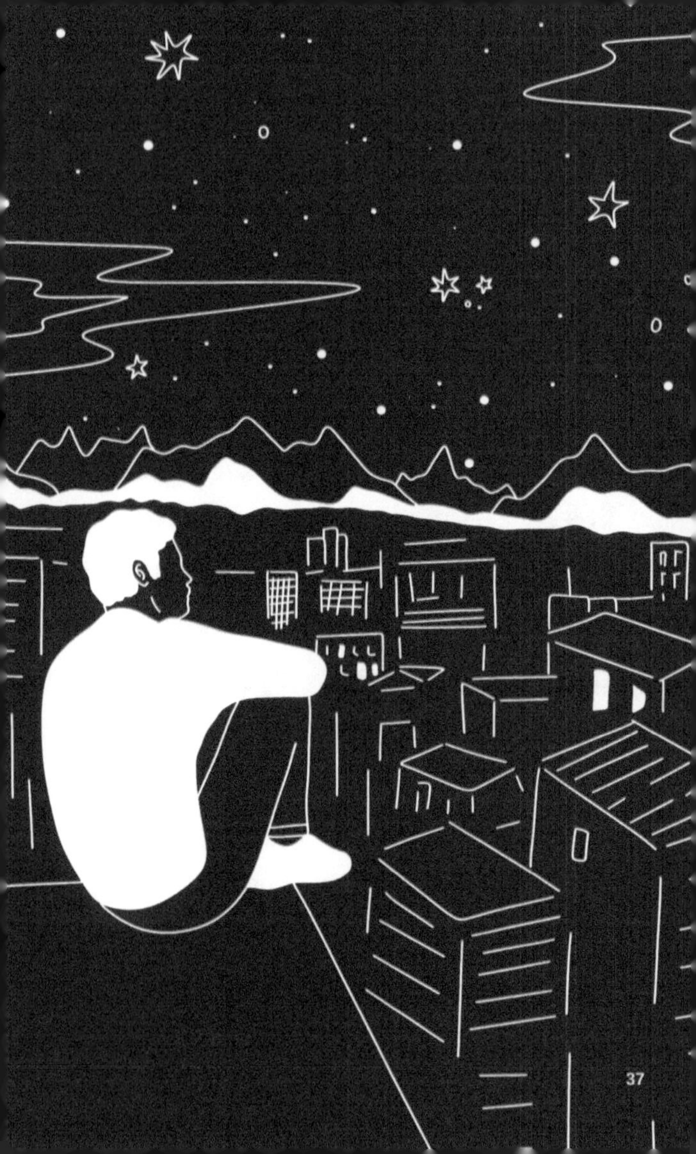

i sit above the noise
of near-empty city streets
and watch the dim lights
fade and bounce
announce themselves
one last time
before they leave –
returning home

[rooftop after dark]

23-05-05
3:1111 EST
43.6517° N, 79.3825° W

i love it when the power goes
and no one knows quite what to say
the night has never been so long
and our foreign song fills the air
reaching out into the dark
with a faint and vulnerable remark
powerless in a different way
as we say things we never say
we hear each other for the first time
as our hearts begin to rhyme

[blackout]

08-144
16:11 EDᵀ
43.6535° N, 79.3830° W

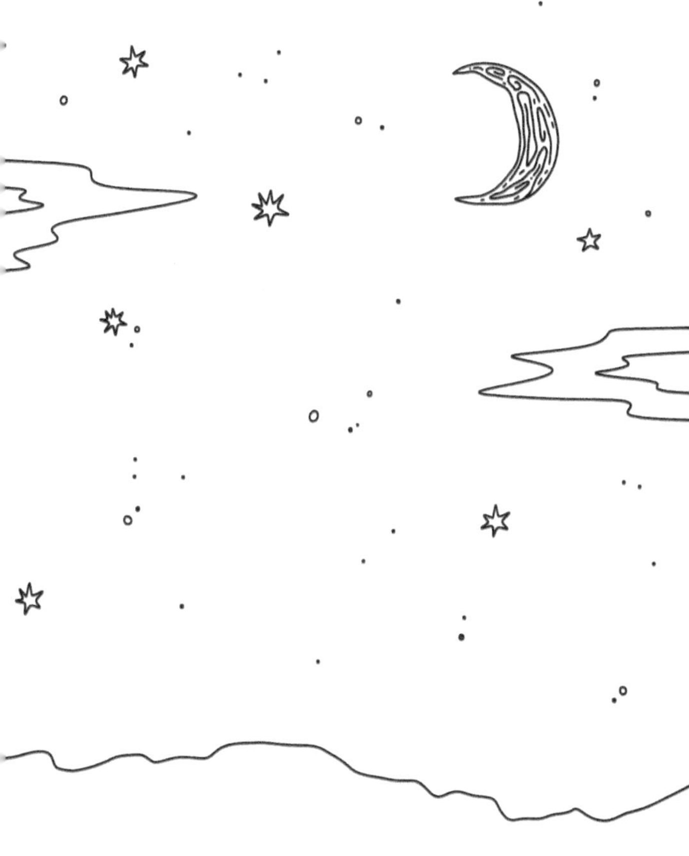

it's the little things that stay with me now:

i remember the decrepit apartment above the
laundromat

i remember how we managed to find love
there for the first time

i remember how it felt to fall asleep beneath
the crooked ceiling fan and pretend that our
dreams weren't just dreams

i remember how it was always a little cold
and a little damp and how the white noise of
the dehumidifier would lull us to sleep

i remember how nothing was bothersome
then

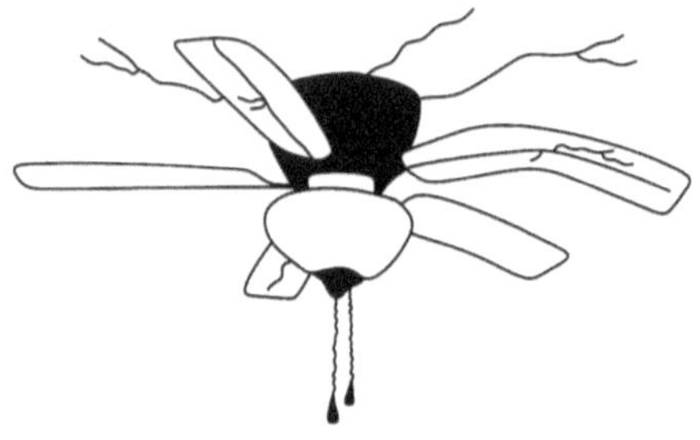

you never need much at first do you?

a single bed perhaps
a sturdy floor
and a slow
deep slumber
under the trapped light
of too many stars —

do you remember when
this was enough to
keep our love?

[nostalgia in the city]

10-30 -12
22:66 EST
43. 16° N, 79.3817° W
   46

tracing my fingers along the spines
of weathered artifacts
i am brought back to a time
when you and i
quite different from now
would explore great worlds
both fact and fiction
and dream up ways
to capture moments
and try to stop the time
from passing us by

[where we used to be]

12-12-23
15:45 EST
43.6677° N, 79.3948° W

i call to you softly sometimes
when i am alone
just to feel the words on my tongue
to taste you again
through rituals of life
in moments of rest
through coffee cups

i whisper

spinning spoons
like a trance
the aroma of life
rises to my lips
and i say your name

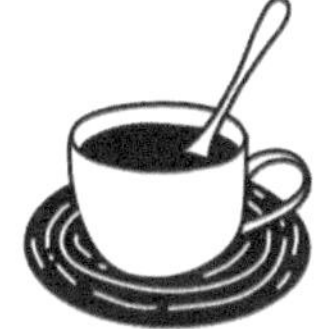

[ruminating]

11-03-24
07:12 EST
43.6541° N, 79.3830° W

you come to me
like a wave
all at once
i am overcome
by the feeling
that i have
known you
all my life

06-18-16
19:30 EST
43.6475° N, 79.3° W

this memory
is too heavy
and hard to hold
but it is all
i have left

04-12 25
02:47 EST   38
43.6723' N, 79.3831° W

my hand stretches out to touch cold air
and in the blackest part of night
my fingers curl back
as my heart falls once more
inside my chest

there is no foundation here

but i cannot stop myself
from reaching for you

1-07-97 EST
2:13 EST1°   N, 79.3470° ° W
3.6511° N, 79.3470° W

i can still remember
the way the evening sun
would cast a golden shadow
on our love
through the shades
onto the floor
your body
bathed in light
where we were

[sunday]

12-14-97
19:05 EST
43.6511° N, 79.3470° W

the hardest part about losing love
is that life goes on

he thought

he stayed out all night again
overwrought
missing her

the sun has just peered out
from beneath the moon
and the pavement is still cool
from the night's last shadow

he is waiting for something to happen
but nothing ever does
he longs for how it was
but this is life most days
without her now

everything is still turning

just turning

05-23-24
05:10 EST
43.6545° N, 79.3880° W

today i saw a lilac cat
with your same colored eyes
and i thought to myself
how lovely it was
and if i had nine lives
i would choose to love you
in all of them

04-29-18
16:42 EST
43.6... 79.3957° W

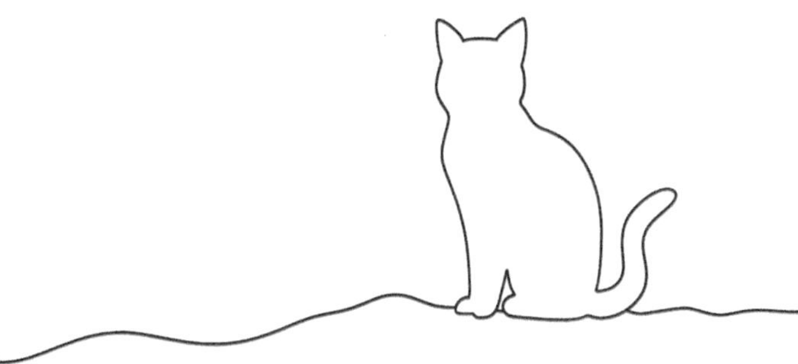

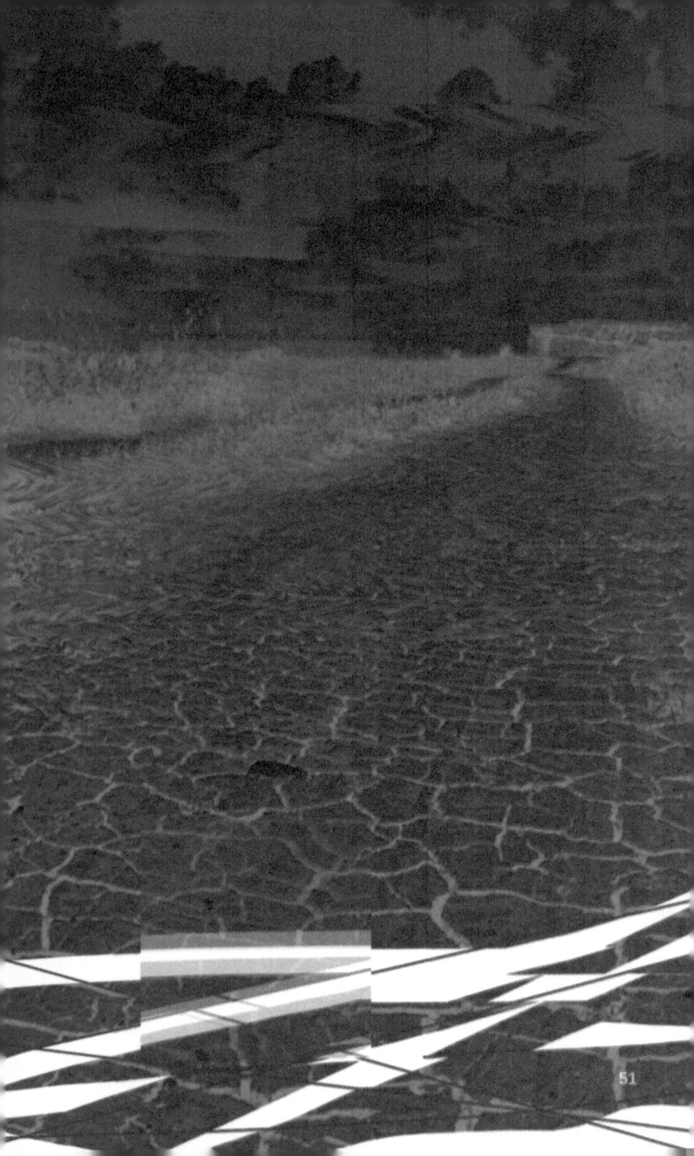

there are cracks in the ground
where we used to lie in warmth
but these crevices are seeded with truth
and baptized by hard rain
so come spring they will bear flowers
and at last reveal the earnest truth
that we often see growth
in all the places that have been broken

[fault lines]

03-16-25
14:27 EST
43.6693° N, 79.3948° W

you are not that young
but also not that old
you are between chapters
waiting to unfold

so stay here wanting for a while
and let nostalgia take its turn
but if you dwell here for too long
the memories will burn

your eyes have witnessed
your true path
and you can't turn away
so rest a bit
the journey is long
tomorrow's a new day

[moving day]

09-17-99
18:03 EST
43.6679° N, 79.3941° W

shopping malls at 6am
and discotheques at noon
stock markets on holidays
and ski resorts in june
a red-eye flight at sunrise
a vacant summer school
a grocery store at closing
an empty motel pool
a playground in the winter
a beach just after rain

a faint

distorted

echoed voice

announcing the last train

[rare aesthetic]

06-03-93
23:59 EST
43.°15° N, 79.4103° W

the flowers by my bedside
must have something to say
because somehow
they still face the light
when wilted
dead
and gray

maybe in the end
they recalled their vibrant youth
and basked in sunshine in their hearts
and realized deeper truth

so when it's our last goodbye
i hope we won't be sad
and like the daisies on the sill
let memories make us glad

[seasons in the sun]

09-12-21
07:4' 45'ST
38.8 89 ° N, 77.036

TRAVEL AND NATURE...

watchingasyouleavef
o...surrealswirlsofmid
niightstars...youdidth
ebestyoucould...there
isnothingtobefound...
donotfolloowyourhea
rtttt...betweenthefall
andwiinter...whydidyo
uhavetoenditallthetii
meyou...wewereneveri
nthesametime....betw
eenthespacesof...alltt
hethingsimeanttosay
before...takemewithy
ouwhenyouleaveee...il
lneverbethesameasth

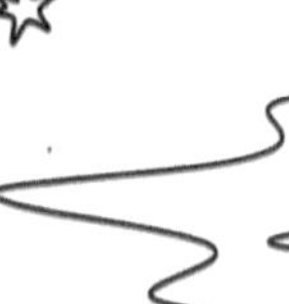

nothing is as it seems...

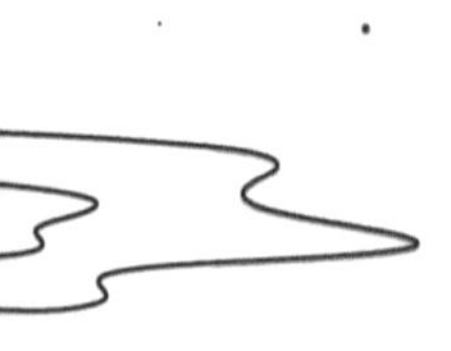

between the earth and sunrise
i stand in awe of night
and teeter on the precipice
of my own fragile light
who am i to be here
to witness this delight
how dare i gaze at galaxies
or marvel at this sight

my eyes are not so worthy
my bones will soon be dust
but something calling
seems to say:

these wonders are a must

maybe it's my duty
just to see and not be seen
maybe it's the only purpose
there has ever been

[cosmic awe]

04-14-04
05:30 HST
19.8207° N, 155.4681° W

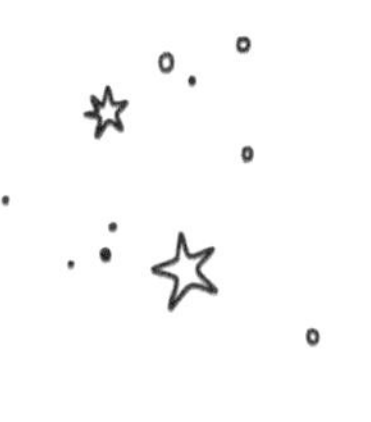

i think it is the saddest thing to know
that leaves in autumn do not ever show
their true colors until they begin to die
perhaps they are a lot like you and i

10-20-22
44.2305° N, 76.4899° W

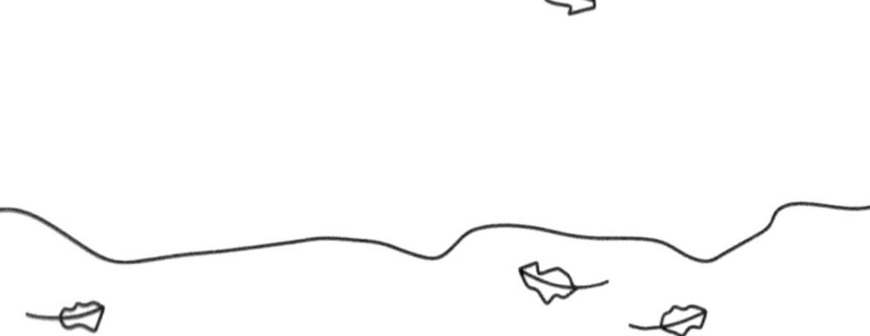

let's do nothing together

sit beneath the trees

visit our favourite park

watch the autumn leaves
glue themselves like paper mache
to the dampened ground

sip something warm from a paper cup
as winter comes around

soon it will be too cold here
to sit and watch and wait
so let's do nothing soon my love
before it gets too late

10-28-22
14:18
:18 EST
44.2305° N, 76.489° W

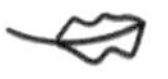

*our love was never
black and white*

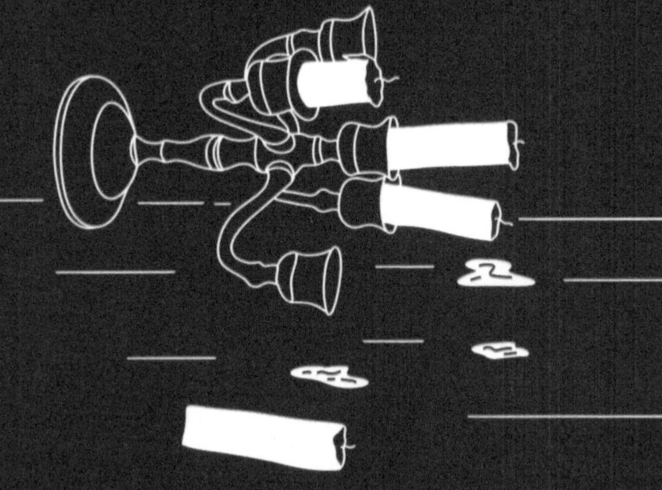

but it was always
more black than white

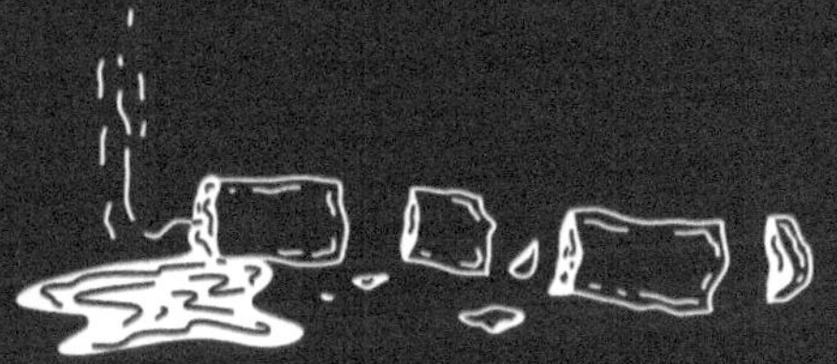

the seasons turn
from green to gold
and in the cold
the crisp air holds
the loose strands
of my auburn hair
as i quietly stare
and think about
when love was new
it's always raining
when i think of you
and i ask myself
now that we're apart:

were we a tragedy
or a work of art?

10-21-24
16:33
45.6333

she transforms darkness into light
and makes beauty out of pain
a fairy lily in the night
that blooms just after rain

[Zephyrlily]

02:18 AM EDT
45.4215° N, 75.6972° W.

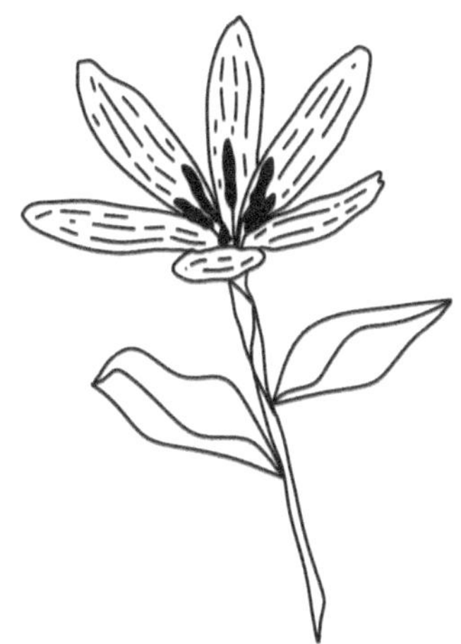

do not follow your heart
if it only calls at night
or breaks through peaceful dreams
just to say:

you're not doing it right

do not follow your heart
if it calls you from your home
to be aimless or to roam
through vast deserts of new beginnings
and countless non-adventures
forsaking all you own
everything you've known
mother
father
brother
wife
loyal friend
all your life

for true adventures are always marked
with beginnings and with ends
and returning to good friends
who see you on and greet you back
from off the lost unbeaten track

it is never a new truth you find
but a tired one as old as time

your heart is a gentle and quiet sound
that will always leave you homeward bound

so if you are being forced
down steep valleys and up sharp peaks
do not follow your heart
it is not your heart that speaks

[note to self]

22:41 EST
43.6532° N, 79.3832° W

i visit your memory everyday
as if you had some way of knowing
the longing grows inside of me
like the swell of a lonely sea
but with no shores to wash upon
like the tidal wave at dawn
i swallow myself again

05-11-14
05:16 AST
45.2730° N, 66.0630° W

a swirl of light
some golden stars
a moonlit night
a love like ours

easy to hold
but hard to keep
we were lost before
we went to sleep

the years did race
so i came to see
the very place
i last felt free

but the gilded lights
were rearranged
and familiar sights
were feeling strange

a lazy breeze
and sea salt air
a glass-top table
a wicker chair

bent and faded
but sturdy too
i breathe the air
and begin anew

06-14-0
15:42 EST
29.2115° N,   273° W

she's a torrent in the ocean
and a whisper on the breeze
she lives in mushroomed mountains
where the wild things sit in ease

she sleeps with spirit foxes
and dances with the moon
she's a galaxy at midnight
and the forest shade at noon

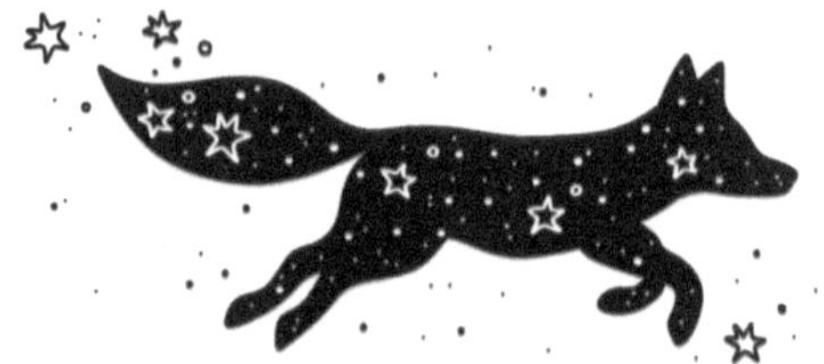

she has the power to inspire awe
and bring you to your knees
you'll find her on the jungle floor
and in its tallest trees

she honors all her nature
especially the garden inside
and if you hear her in the wind
you cannot run and hide

she'll make you see your self
like you've never seen it before
she'll grant you all but what you seek
and leave you wanting more

so offer up your truth
if you ever hear her song
she'll give meaning to your life
and show where you belong

[sublime]

08-   23
    -09-
06:        JST
06::33
31.5935° N, 130.5570° E

is there anything more peculiar
than when nature herself
is out of season

03-12-24
10:17 EST.
44.0376° N, 76.2501° W

i think of you when i look at the stars
not because they are bright
or brave
or pure
or magic

but because they were there
when we were there

and each endless night
that engulfed our love
was pinned to my heart

over again

i think of you when i look at the stars
because now they are all that is left

[the heavens were our witness]

08-17-23
22:02 EST
44.3121° N, 76.4678° W

sitting here beneath the january sky
the crystal branches cry
weeping under the weight
of nature's frozen kiss
and all at once in this
i am both heaviness and light
and overwhelmed and right
as i breathe the quiet air
a snowy owlet's stare
and the steadiness
of my own solitary breath
is all that is there

[ice storm]

01-01-14
09:00 EST
43.7708° N, 79.2545° W

in this uninhabitable place
you gave all of yourself to love
the only way you knew how
do not think that it went unnoticed

[karma]

10-03-23
02:47 EST
4.[illegible]° N, 76.51[illegible]7° W

LOVE BETWEEN SPACES...
i'llneverunderstandw
htyoumeant...we'vego
ttonight...bluelightsf
adingoverthecity.....in
mydreamsiiseeyourfa
ce...yousaidforeveran
daday.....coffeeeeshop
sssandplaceswhere...
sometimesirecall...it'
sneeverasgoodthesec
ontimearound...howm
anytimesdoihavetofal
lb...whenthemoonisfu
llandbright.....howstar
kistheday...iremembe
reverythiingasifitwer

as i kissed
the last frost of winter
from your lashes
late that february evening
the snow turned to rain
and i thought to myself
how funny it was
that in a mere
matter of moments
a stranger could grow
to mean so much

[platform 9]

02-19-24
18:41 EST
43.6452° N, 79.3806° W

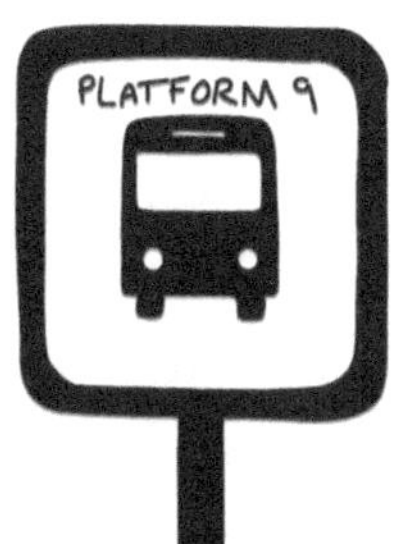

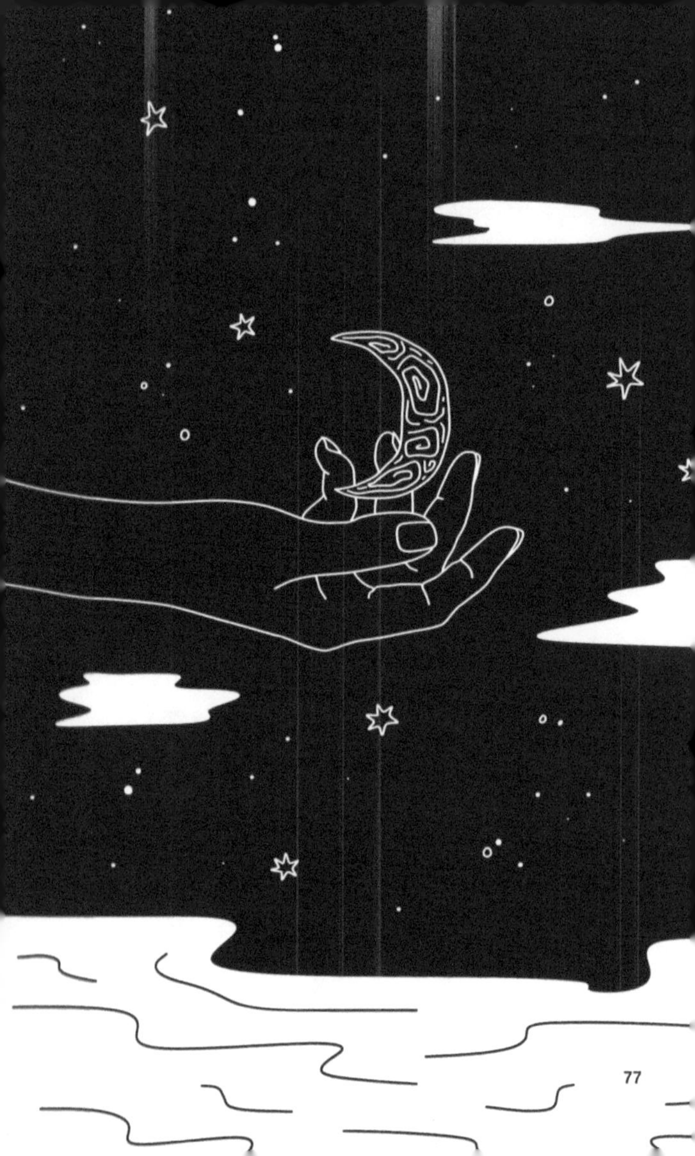

it was just about june
when the morning moon
kissed the pond
and i grew quite fond
of the way that your shoes
of sapphire blues
remained on the shore
askew by the door
always next to mine

[routein]

06-10-24
05:23 EST
44.2338° N, 76.6178° W

in our house
there will be an old window
not the type that leaks
or lets in the cold air
the sturdy kind
of many panes
the sort you would imagine
has held in the warmth
of a dozen lifetimes
and immeasurable love

it will keep us safe
and shield us from the storm
all our lives

11.05-23
16.57 EST
44.2292° N, 76.4818° W

i think of you at the beginning of every day
i still see your face at the end of every night
in the spaces between
when there's no one around
when there isn't a sound
but the beating of my restless heart
so when we're apart
and you find yourself reaching for me
across the sea of this separation
you can meet me in that place
where it is always dusk
and always dawn
where memory lives
you will find me there
in the shadow of life
in the remains of the day

i never left

04-12-24
19:37 EST
2 .7 17° N, 8 18° W

i'd write of stardust in your eyes
or flowers that bloom in arid dirt
but you my love are more alive
in every way more down to earth

i cannot touch you in the sky
or reach across a vast dead sea
so i will meet you eye to eye
and you can stay in love with me

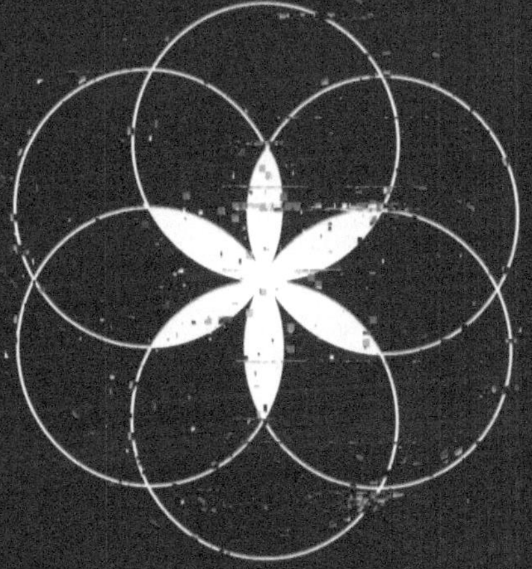

i glow deep and dim
i suppose that's what lured you in
nothing earth-shattering at first
this kind of love is never a burst of lightning
just a familiar song
a reminder of the wrong in me
i tried to leave behind

it's an echo that disturbs the peace
and will not cease until it's had its turn

so i wasn't surprised
to find you on that eve
washed up on the bank
as i sank into myself
for the very first time

[star-crossed - her p.o.v]

there you were
beneath the moon
a familiar tune
waiting
wanting
hiding
luring me
like a ship at sea
somehow i knew though i had no view
it was as if my whole life
was leading me to the moment
when i would say your name
for the very first time

[star-crossed - his p.o.v]

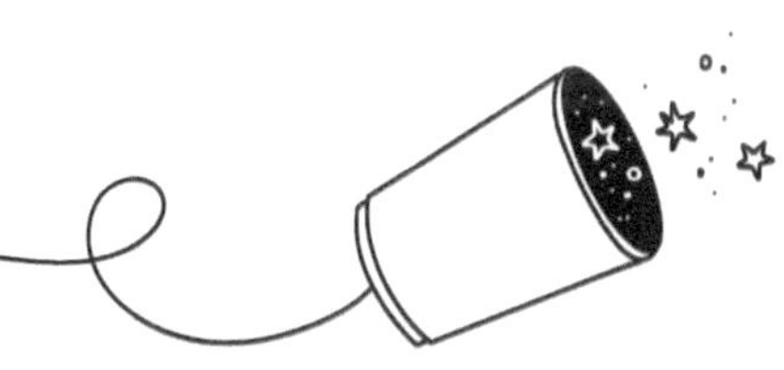

how

many

times

do

i

have

to

fall

before

i

learn

to

follow

through

07-14-24
0:08 AST
44.4920° N, 63.9187° W

i cannot love you too brightly
in the morning sun
else you grow suspicious
that i might want this
more than you know
so i will hold on tightly
only while you sleep
and every night
you will be mine
and i will be yours
and we will be love

[secret love]

08-22-21
02:33 E T
43.6575° N, 79.3832° W

i can still recall the bright april morning
when i was still light with longing
before the weight of love filled my being
for the very first time

now there is a heaviness
i will always choose to carry

this sacred burden
this thankless promise
this unconditional desire
has given my life meaning
where there once was none

04-14-24
08:21 EST
43.6510° N, 79.____° W

your love is worth the wait
and worth the weight

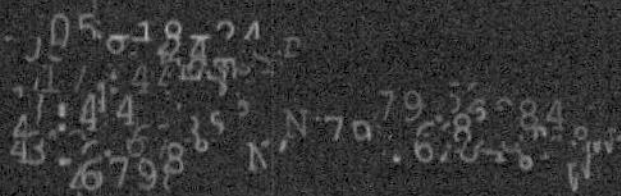

the light is blue and so am i
as evening falls upon the sky
i breathe you in with one last sigh
darkness calls
the stars
they spy
and tell a tale of passers-by
the end of love is drawing nigh
the light is blue and so am i

[ultraviolet]

06-21-24
06-21-24
20:49 EST
20:49 EST
43.9070° N, 77.2392° W
43.9070° N, 77.2392° W

when i said forever
i only meant it if you stayed

there is too much time now

forever is too long
if you are not here

10-0/-284
2(43.3 EST
43.9070° N, 77.2392° W

take me with you when you leave
i'll keep you safe and warm
let me live inside your heart
let me take its form

i wished so much that you could stay
and that fate would make a vow
but i know that you must go
so i'll say goodbye for now

i hope your journey is as wide
and vast as every sea
i hope you find the thing you seek
and that it lives in me

07-15.16
06:08 EST
44.2372° N, 76.5368° W

there are so many things
i wanted to say in the end

but more than anything

i want you to know that
i'm not mad at you for leaving

i'm not mad at you for choosing
your happiness over mine

because i will always choose
your happiness over mine

you and me
we are the same

19:34 EST
51.0447° N, 114.0719° W

....couldyoufallasleept
othesoundofmyv...the
resastoryaboutuswaii
tingto...voicesfromth
evoidandthe...stillnes
sisthequalityi....thelo
ngestdayofmylifewas
nothingto...howamisu
pposedto...theshadow
siinthehallwayof...doy
ounoticthelittlething
satallo...willyoumaket
herightchoicewhenth
etimecomes...it's1995
...youhavenot...youare
tooold....letsbeginnnn

my dear
you are far too deep
to be drowning
in such shallow waters

take a second look
at your reflection in the tide
try not to hide
your true feelings anymore
dig your heels into the sand
and remind yourself
that you know how to stand

17:26 EST
44.0115° N, 77.2148° W

sleep now
soon it will be
the season of transformation
a chapter to recall
that everything must perish
in order to begin anew
so rest a while
and let this slow autumn haze
turn you over again
and enter the world of dreams

[september]

09-22-25
17:26 EST
44.2293° N, 76.4883° W

the longest day
you'll ever have
will be the one
where you begin
your new life
in the ruins
of the old

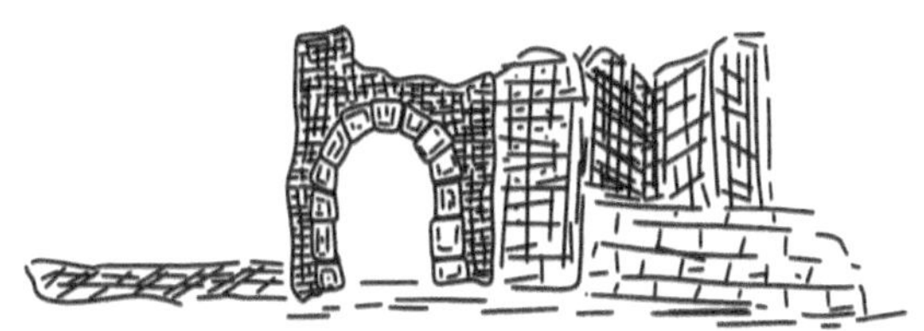

you have a right
to rites of passage

08-21-24
18:15 EST
44.2311° N, 76.4808° W

as you ascend
the palace stairs
remember
the same path
that leads you up
can also lead you down

[why we bow to take the crown]

she lives in black unholy tides
where nothing sleeps and nothing hides
beneath the shadow of the moon
a place where lovers drown too soon
the pool is dim and never deep
its whispers haunt her in her sleep
and calls her to the shore at night
to wash off any morning light

[dark shallow pool]

10-02-24
23:18 EST
44.2334° N, 76.4930° W

if i peeled you an orange
would you notice me

how about a cup of tea
what if i made a pot for two
we could even watch it brew together
as we sat and laughed
seeing all the nature
pass at the window sill

if i mentioned the beautiful bill
on the morning bird
would you hear a single word

or would you miss me as you do
because of your careless and narrow view
as you wondered in an idle flash
who left the fruit peel in the trash

[bird test]

08-28-24
09:14 EST
43.6575° N, 79.3782° W

you ask me why i keep coming back
and i don't really have an answer
perhaps it's the fear you put in me
that grows like silent cancer

you told me i'll never be enough
and like some sort of charity case
i'm lucky you even gave me a chance
and showed me this merciful grace

so i sit and wait each time you leave
for you to change your mind
and every "sorry" i believe
in hopes that you will find
some evidence i deserve your love
because how could you be so blind

you ask me why i keep coming back
i can find no reason or rhyme
i guess the truth is i never left
i've been here the entire time

[on again/off again]

09-05-24
20:11 EST   .91
44.4917° N, 63.9187° W

i felt a knot in my stomach
at the dawn of our love
because i knew that night
would soon settle in
and reveal to us
all that is not visible
in the light

04-07-24
05:32 EST
44.4939° N, 63.914 0° W

amid the hidden sentiments
of life's deepest promise
he sits and waits

wandering with purpose
along the edges

the elusive
must be left to fly

paths are long on this circular road

faith sets in
and the heart
awaits a return

09-12-24
07:05 EST.
43.6625° N, 79.3950° W

today i thought
i saw your shadow
the memory of you
crept its way
through my door
up the stairs
and into my bed

it was a solemn comfort

a reminder of what we once were

i wonder

is it really your ghost
that's haunting me
or are you still alive

[haunted]

09-18-24
21:43 EST
43.6578° N, 79.3945° W

i grab the nearest apple
and i crush it with my teeth
these hanging fruit are sweet
i search hungrily for another
it is already at my feet
now easier to reach
i stoop to meet its level
lying on the floor
it collapses in my grip
it is rotted to the core

[low-hanging fruit]

025-24.24
14:    5° N,   79
43.6626   79.3953° W

,

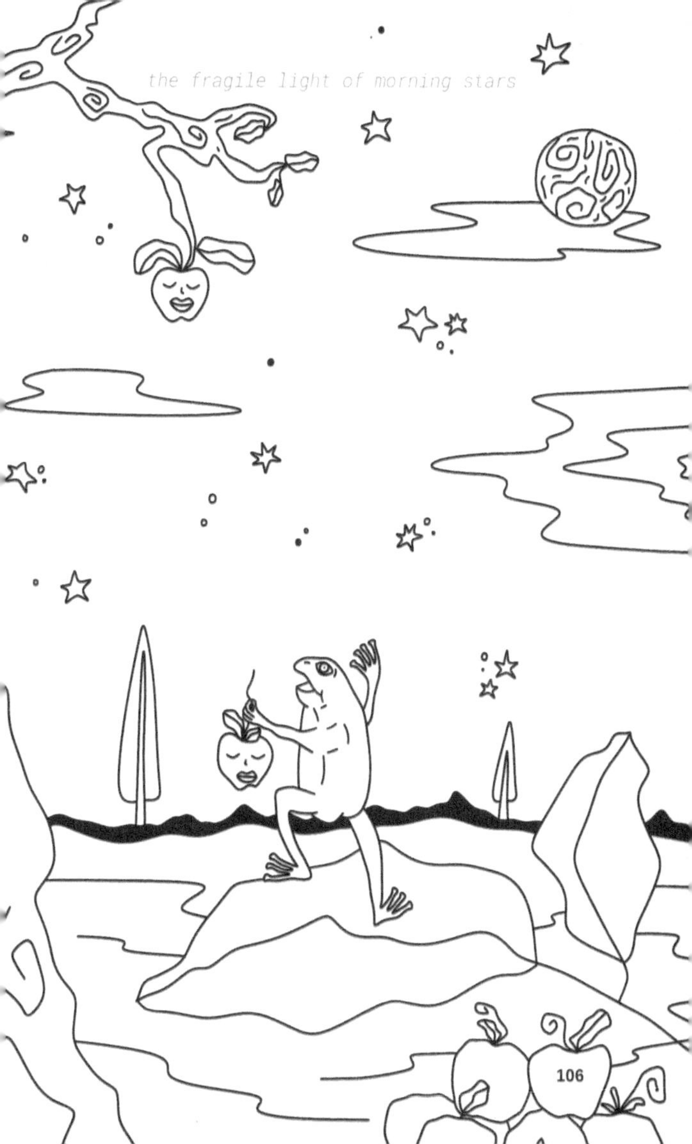
the fragile light of morning stars
106

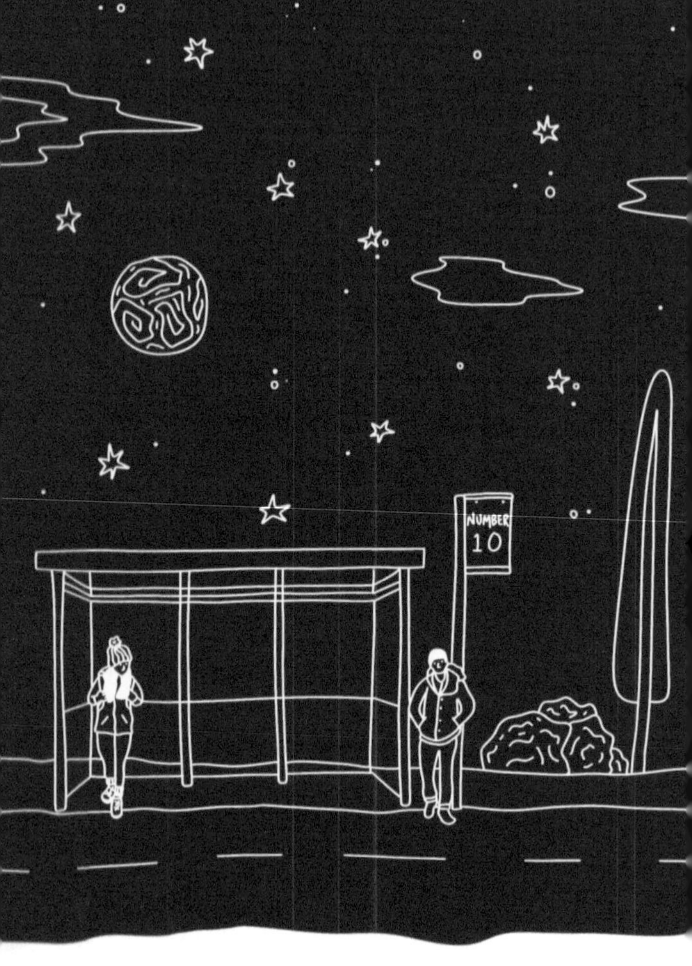

NUMBER
10

something has been lost
in the way that the frost
lingers in the air
between your breath and mine
while the dim sunshine
falls off the bay
and seems to say
the day is done
though we haven't begun
to see the change
we only feel a little strange

[the beginning of the end]

11:45 EST
16.2338
44.2338° N, 76.617° W

you'll know that your love is finally over
the day that your life changes for the better
and you have no desire to write them a long
letter telling them about it

instead you'll take that diary scrap
and shape it into a paper boat
and send it to float to the lost isle of your
heart

a fresh start

and then one day
you will meet someone new
who loves you as much
as you used to love them
and every rose will wither off its stem
because you no longer press them into a book
you no longer take a second look

there is nothing left to say
and you had no choice
but to walk away

10-14-24
16:41 EST
43.6467° N,   3745° W
79

i was also cold on the day you died
i hope you'll forgive my sin
i already grieved before the change
in the colour of your skin
i cannot tell whether i am numb
or finally at peace
now that you're gone
will the mourning start
or will it finally cease

[grim]

:1-03-24
43.7042° N 79.3981° W

fingers reaching wildly
like naked trees to an endless sky
lonely hearts are aching
under harvest moons held high

she dreamt of making a bed
inside of someone else's home
but that was just a plot
for feeling evermore alone

so beneath these stark white shadows
she will let her longing cease
and reach inside her self
to find her heart at last at peace

[alone but not lonely]

10-17-24
22:11 EST
43.6897° N, '79.2962° W

i do not like
clean lines or smooth edges
i like life best
with a bit of patina on it
the cracks
are how the light gets in
as they say
so give me all the spaces
between the lines
and i will dance
and live in truth

[rustic life]

1-27-24
8
38:36 EST
3:
.6502° N, 79.3729° W

i had tea with my inner child last night
because neither of us could sleep
she sat at my small kitchen table
as i put our favourite brew to steep

she was fidgeting and swaying
like a flame that was hard to contain
eyes sharp with questions
but lips pressed tight
she could tell that i knew her pain

she measured me as she tilted her head
and in the way that she squinted her eyes
[guarded] because she thought i would say
"you're too much" but to her surprise
i laughed instead because i recall
how i once carried myself bottled up
i told her that things would soon be alright
as she sipped nervously from her cup

i remember how we held a light for those
who only reached for it when they had none
so i told her that she would not find a home
in the rays of a dying sun

i told her instead one day she would learn
how to live without shrinking away

and that she would be known
without needing to be
a part of herself
just to stay

you will sit at tables where no one leaves
and in rooms where no one will flinch
you will speak without shaking
and live without breaking
and your home will be safe
[every inch]

she exhaled and then took a pause
like she had been holding her breath
in for years
and we sipped our tea in silence
all at once feeling like peers

it's a kind of knowing that soothes your soul
like the unison voice of a choir
between two people who've walked the same
path through the baptismal fire

[midnight chai]

11-15-24
3:04 EST
43.6699° N, 79.3947° W
7

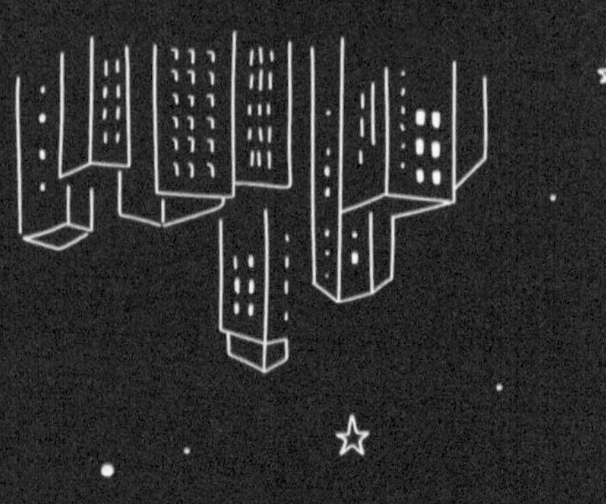

some comforts are too comfortable

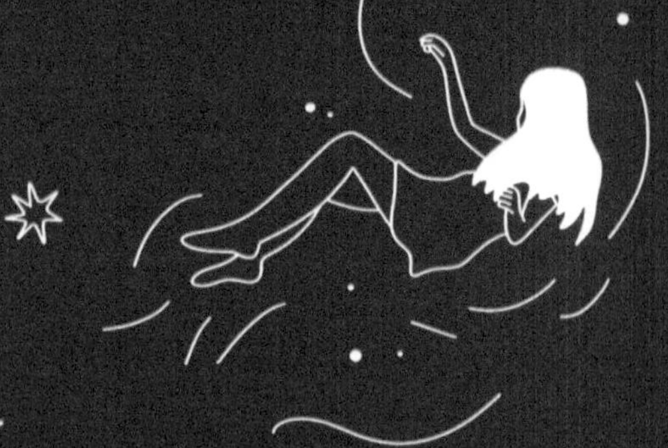

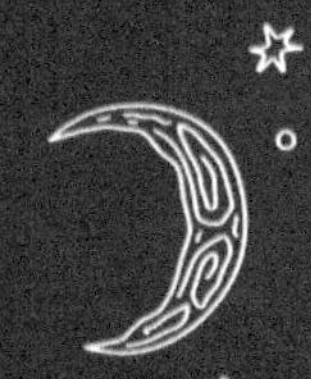

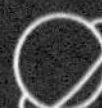

find comfort in the uncomfortable

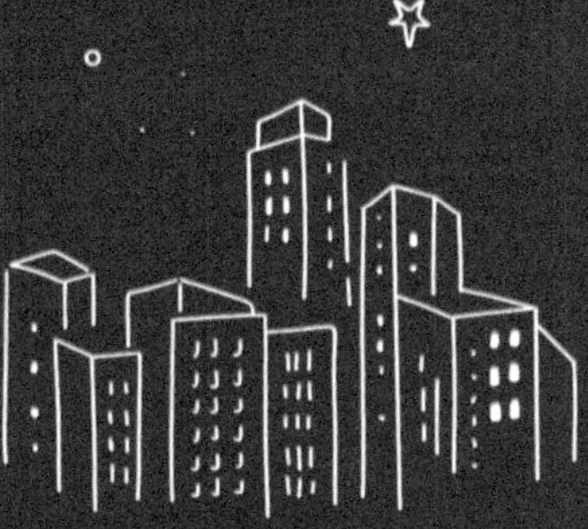

I am change
what I felt yesterday
I do not feel today
and what I am today
I will not be tomorrow
but I will live my life
with conviction
every hour
trusting that
no matter the circumstance
my average dealing
will equal truth

[becoming]

the flowers in your hair
may have fallen to the ground
scattered here and there
never to be found again
but they have left their truth
along your weary path
and in their aftermath
seed the promise of yesterday's deeds
and wait in the weeds
to grant that you will bloom tomorrow

[experience]

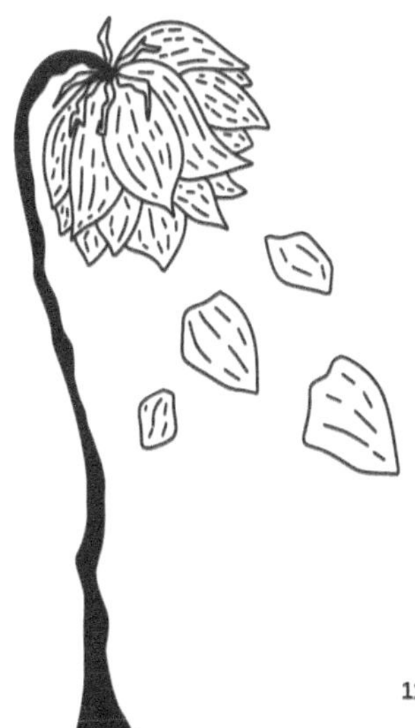

thank you for being.

www.ingramcontent.com/pod-product-compliance
Lightning Source LLC
Chambersburg PA
CBHW031346060726
47590CB00007B/2648